This Book Belongs To:

How to use this coloring book:

Rule #1: Have fun. This book is meant to make you smile, laugh, & have a good time with friends. It's for the love of all things Kawaii!

Rule #2: You can scan and print individual page images for personal use so you can color an image more than once, or to share with friends. You're allowed to scan images for coloring digitally too. For extra durability, you can laminate your bookmark; it'll last longer!

Rule #3: Be creative and give finished works away as super fun gifts. To aid with cutting, use a ruler and a sharp knife to remove pages. Make sure you have an adult's help!

Rule #4: Please do not post uncolored pages on-line or sell any images for profit, colored or not. You are encouraged to show off your colored images as much as you want though, as well as show photos or video for book review purposes!

Rule #5: Refer to Rule #1 & enjoy!

*Kawaii:
-said like Hawaii, but with a "k," means "cute" in Japanese.

Red Panda

Flamingos

Giraffe & Meerkat

Moth & Caterpillar

Bearded Dragon
& Cricket

Bear

Sloth

Sea Turtles

Armadillo
& Ant

Snow Leopard

Stingrays

Rattlesnake

Kangaroo

Chameleon

Platypus & Catfish

Jumping
Spider

Puma/Cougar

Humpback Whale & Pelican

Cockatoo

Hyena

Hermit Crab & Starfish

Bumble Bee

Walrus

Kiwi

Horse

Test Color Page